Nelson

Spelling

Developing Skills

John Jackman

3

BOOK THREE

Scottish Adviser: Iain Campbell

D1628034

CONTENTS/SCOPE AND SEQUENCE

Page	Focus	Extra	Extension	Focus resource	Extension resource
34/35 Unit 14 soft c	wordsearch puzzle	-ice words puzzle	-ace words fan; alphabetical ordering	-ice -ace letter patterns / word sums	alphabetical ordering
36/37 Unit 15 homophones	selecting key words	matching homophones	mnemonics	identifying correct homophone	selecting homophones
38/39 Unit 16 unstressed vowels	wordsearch puzzle	spotting unstressed vowels; correcting spellings	syllables	identifying unstressed vowels	identifying unstressed vowels; syllables
40/41 Unit 17 ost oll	matching picture clues; rhyme activity	letter patterns -oll, -oal, -ole	adding all or al	making -ost -oll words	adding missing l or ll
42/43 Unit 18 same letters different sound	rhyming activity	sorting ea words by sound	sorting ear and ough words by sound	making rhyming words	sorting ough words by sound
44/45 Unit 19 using a dictionary	alphabetical ordering	using a dictionary	guide words	alphabetical ordering	guide words
46/47 Check-up 2	*Check-up 2*	*Check-up 2*	*Check-up 2*	*Check-up 2*	*Check-up 2*
48/49 Unit 20 un en in im	matching picture clues	in- en- un- dictionary quiz	adding prefixes that double a letter	matching definitions	adding prefixes
50/51 Unit 21 soft g	matching picture clues	-age wordsearch	nge words puzzle	matching picture clues	definitions; wordsearch activity
52/53 Unit 22 ie	key words wordsearch	plurals of -f and -fe words	word webs	-ief word fan	ie / ei rule practice
54/55 Unit 23 ei	matching picture clues; wordsearch	ie / ei rule	ei homophones	-eigh letter pattern / word sums	jumbled words; homophones
56/57 Unit 24 ey endings	identifying ey letter patterns; ey puzzle	making plurals of words ending in y	making plurals	-ey -ney -key letter patterns; wordsearch	-y word plurals
58/59 Unit 25 ild ind	cloze activity; identifying letter patterns	homonyms	adding prefixes and suffixes	-ild -ind letter patterns / word sums	adding prefixes and suffixes
60/61 Unit 26 -e or -e̶?	matching key words; adding ing	adding ing to magic e words	adding vowel and consonant suffixes	+ing word sums	word fans adding suffixes
62/64 Check-up 3	*Check-up 3*	*Check-up 3*	*Check-up 3*	*Check-up 3*	*Check-up 3*

OCUS

A What are these? The letters will give you a clue.
Write the words in your book.

1 b _____

2 g _____

3 r _____

4 l _____

5 _____ f

6 s _____

7 m _____

8 b _____

9 l _____

10 b _____

11 k _____

12 s _____

13 h _____

14 _ l _____

15 _____ t _____

16 _____ t

B Copy and complete these word sums in your book.

1 all + so =   2 all + though =

C Copy these pairs of words. Underline the root, circle any prefixes in red and any suffixes in blue.

1 unconscious   consciously
2 cautioned   precautionary

A Copy and complete these word sums in your book.

1 lap + ing =   2 clap + ed =

3 employ + ment =   4 happy + ness =

5 victory + ous =   6 wolf + s =

7 stroke + ing =   8 pass + s =

B Write a homophone for each of these words.

1 lone   2 fair   3 threw   4 here

C Add **able** or **ible** to finish these words.

1 imposs _____   2 unsuit _____   3 illeg _____

EXTENSION

A Write these words in alphabetical order.

1 trace   train   tractor   transfer   traffic

B Copy the words and next to each write the suffix or suffixes.

1 neighbourliness   2 attractive   3 helpfully

C Add **en** or **n** to each word to make another word from the same family.

1 broke   2 wake   3 bright   4 fall   5 shake

D Use a dictionary to help you make the abstract noun to go with each of these verbs.

1 distract   2 impress   3 operate   4 attend   5 explore

ar
are

Be sm**ar**t! Cross with c**are**.
Stop for c**ar**s. Be aw**are**!

FOCUS

KEY WORDS

bark
barn
cart
smart
start

care
rare
fare
aware
beware
scare
spare
stare
share

A Look at these picture clues.
Write the **ar** or **are** words in your book.

1 c_____ 2 c_____ 3 s_____

4 sh_____ 5 sc_____ 6 st_____

B Copy these words neatly into your book.

ark park spark sparkle sparkler sparklers

Write a sentence to explain what you notice about their spellings.

Sort the key words into sound pattern families and write them in your book, like this:

words with _ar_ sounding like c_ar_	words with _are_ sounding like c_are_
barn	fare

Add two more words of your own to each list.

XTENSION

A Put one suffix on each word, without changing any spellings, like this:
care + fully = carefully

You need to think very **carefully**!

word box	suffix box
care	ly
art	ing
start	er
scare	fully
smart	ful
bark	d

B Write sentences using three of the words you have made.

word roots

actor act action

KEY WORDS

act
actor
action
activity

port
portable
porter
export
import
report

scribe
scribble
manuscript
describe

A Sort the words in the box into word families.
There are five families with three words in each family.

> medic relation children medicine childhood
> cover childish discovery impressive recover
> expression press relate medication relatively

B Add at least one more word yourself to each family group.

 XTRA

Copy these words into your book. Make as many family words as you can. The prefixes and suffixes in the box might be helpful. The first one is done to help you.

Remember, a **prefix** is added to the start of a word and a **suffix** is added to the end of a word.

| un in re im en over de dis pre |
| ing ed ly ful ment en ness |

1 joy   enjoy   joyful   enjoying   enjoyment   enjoyable   enjoyed

2 take   3 pain   4 electric

 XTENSION

gradual
dictate fracture
speedometer
contradict
hydraulic
decimal duet
duotone
fraction decade
grade graphic
hydrant
autograph
thermometer

Many words we use in English today came originally from Greek or Latin. Here are some Greek and Latin words with their meanings.

Greek words	
deka	ten
graphein	to write
hydor	water
metron	measure

Latin words	
dictatum	to say or tell
duo	two
frangere	to break
gradus	a step

A Write each of these Greek and Latin words in your book as a list.

Next to each word write the two English words from the box that have been derived from these words.

B Write a simple definition of what each of these Greek and Latin words probably meant. Next to each write some English words that use these roots. The first one is done to help you.
Use a dictionary to help if you wish.

	meaning	uses in English words
magnus	great or large	magnitude, magnify
navis		
octo		
phone		
aqua		

ir
ire

The **Fire**bird
by Stravinsky

Th**ir**d and final
performance

For tickets
enqu**ire** at the
box office.

FOCUS

KEY WORDS

bird
third
shirt
skirt
first
thirsty
fire
wire
retire
inspire
expire
squire
enquire

Look at these picture clues.
Write the **ir** words in your book.

1 st_____ 2 b _____ 3 sp_____

4 f_____ 5 th_____ 6 sk_____

Sort the key words into sound pattern families and write them in your book, like this:

words with _ir_ sounding like f_ir_	words with _ire_ sounding like f_ire_
bird	wire

Add two more words of your own to each list.
Write a sentence using one word from each family.

EXTENSION

Use a dictionary to help you.

a	c	q	u	i	r	e	s	u	j
g	d	e	s	i	r	e	q	h	j
b	m	n	g	t	r	x	u	n	g
t	h	q	i	n	s	p	i	r	e
f	n	u	b	w	r	i	r	a	h
s	h	i	r	e	e	r	e	x	g
f	c	r	n	v	d	e	q	b	g
c	p	e	r	s	p	i	r	e	d

A Make a list of the eight **ire** words hidden in the word box.
Write a definition for each one in your book.
The first one is done for you.

squire – a county gentleman

B Sort the words in your list into alphabetical order.

auto
circum

The pop star is **auto**graphing his **auto**biography.
Under the **circum**stances, I thought there would be more people!

OCUS

KEY WORDS

autograph
automatic
automation
autopsy
autobiography
automobile

circumference
circumnavigate
circumstance
circumvent
circle
circus
circular
circulation

A Look at these picture clues.
Match a key word to each.

1 _____   2 _____   3 _____

4 _____   5 _____   6 _____

B Write three sentences. Each sentence must use one of the key words from A.

EXTRA

Use a dictionary to help you.

A Copy each of these words and next to each write the meaning.

1 autograph   2 automatic   3 autobiography
4 automobile   5 circumvent   6 circumference
7 circulation   8 circumnavigate

B From the information in A, write what you think each of these prefixes means.

1 auto

2 circum

EXTENSION

A Match a phrase from the box to each of the phrases below.

circumstantial evidence	autograph book
circumvent the problem	increase the circulation
her fascinating autobiography	the circumference of the object
an automatic machine	

1 the distance around the outer edge
2 sell more copies
3 information that seems to show what happened
4 a collection of interesting signatures
5 get around the difficulty
6 works by itself
7 the interesting book she wrote about her life

B Use two of the phrases in the box in your own sentences.

words ending

a i o u

Can you see the kangaroo
Jumping past the big emu?

KEY WORDS

armadillo
corgi
cuckoo
dingo
emu
gecko
gnu
kangaroo
kiwi
puma
tarantula
buffalo
anaconda

Look at these pictures and clues.
Write the key words in your book.

1 a wild ox from North America

2 a large spider with a deadly bite

3 an Australian animal with a powerful kick

4 an American wildcat

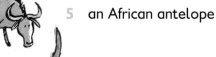

5 an African antelope

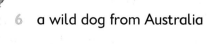

6 a wild dog from Australia

7 a bird named after its call

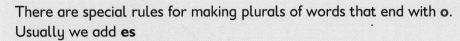

There are special rules for making plurals of words that end with **o**.
Usually we add **es**

tomato   tomato**es**   hero   hero**es**

But we simply add **s** for:
words ending in **oo**   cuckoo**s**
'music' words   piano**s**
shortened words   photo**s**

A Write the plural form of each of these nouns.

1 *tornado*   2 *mango*   3 *cello*   4 *torpedo*

5 *domino*   6 *kangaroo*   7 *cuckoo*   8 *piano*

9 *soprano*   10 *photo*   11 *volcano* 12 *cargo*

B Using a dictionary or other reference books, what can you discover about these words?
Where did they first come from?
Are they a short version of a longer word?

1 photo   2 piano   3 disco   4 rhino   5 hippo

XTENSION

Most of the words we use that end with a vowel letter other than **e** have come from a foreign language.

dahlia bhaji paella banjo spaghetti
emu banana cello chapatti
pasta pizza risotto rosti samosa
macaroni ravioli concerto

A Research the words in the box using dictionaries and other reference books.
1 Sort them into lists according to the countries from which they came.
2 Make a list of the food words.
3 Make a list of the music words.

B The key words are all the names of creatures. Sort them according to the countries or regions from which they come.

y
endings
(nouns)

Cherry berry jelly –
Yucky mucky puppy!

FOCUS

KEY WORDS

jelly

penny

berry

cherry

hobby

puppy

baby

lady

gravy

daisy

ivy

posy

story

A Look at these picture clues.
Write the matching key words in your book.

1 _____ 2 _____ 3 _____

4 _____ 5 _____ 6 _____

B Write the key words that have double letters (like **jelly**) neatly in your book. Next to each write a rhyming word.

C Write a sentence that uses at least two of the key words.

A What am I?

1 I wag my tail when I'm pleased.
2 I grow on bushes.
3 I'm a small bunch of flowers.
4 I'm a tale in a book.
5 I'm a very young child.
6 I wobble a lot!
7 I'm what you do in your spare time.
8 I'm often found climbing trees!

B The words **dairy** and **diary** both end with **y**. What else is interesting about them? Use each in a sentence that shows their meaning.

EXTENSION

Be careful!
The last one
is tricky!

All these nouns end in **y**.
    puppy   story   posy   baby   berry   lady

To make a word plural that ends in a consonant plus **y**, we change the **y** to **i** and add **es**, like this:
    one puppy   three pupp**ies**

Finish these captions. Write the plurals of the words in brackets.

1 two (puppy)_____   2 three (story)_____   3 six (berry)_____

4 three (posy)_____   5 two (baby)_____   6 four (day)_____

dis

I dislike disgusting things like stinky smells and slimy skins.

FOCUS

KEY WORDS

dislike
disobey
disagree
disappear
disbelieve
disconnect
dishonest
distrust
disused
disaster
discover
disease
disgrace
disgusting

A Antonyms are opposites.
Find key words that are the antonyms of each of these words.

1 like   2 agree   3 appear   4 connect
5 honest   6 obey   7 trust   8 believe

What do you notice about all the antonyms?

B Write two sentences using at least two of the other key words.

Here are some dictionary definitions.
Match a word from the box to each one.

> discontent   disappear   discreet   disadvantage
> dislocate   disclose   discard   discharge

1 to pass out of sight
2 something unfavourable, a penalty
3 to throw away
4 to unload/to set free
5 to reveal
6 careful in what one says
7 lack of satisfaction
8 to put out of joint

EXTENSION

Many words with the **dis** pattern are 'negative' words.
This means they are about things which cannot or do not happen, or which are undone.

For example: **dis**trust means **not** to trust
disagree means **not** to agree
disconnect means to **un**do a connection.

There are other negative prefixes, like **de** and **un**.
For example: **de**frost   **un**clear   **un**cover

1 Write five negative words for each of the prefixes **dis**, **de** and **un**
2 Write a definition for each word.

el
endings

travel
camel
kestrel
chisel
gravel
jewel
satchel

F OCUS

KEY WORDS

camel
panel
chapel
gravel
travel
chisel
jewel
novel
cancel
satchel
kestrel
tinsel
hostel
cockerel

A Write the seven key words in the picture above.

B Copy this passage into your book and fill in the missing key words.

A _____ is hovering overhead. It is watching the mouse as it scavenges food from the man's _____. The bird is about to dive when the _____ crows and frightens the mouse, who startles the man, who drops his _____ , just missing the dog, who decides he'll find somewhere more peaceful to sleep!

EXTRA

All the answers to these clues end with the letter pattern **nnel**.

1 You might use this when you wash in the morning.
2 This is a narrow stretch of sea, as between England and France.
3 It's a dog's house you can keep in the garden.
4 It carries roads or railways through mountains.
5 Many ships have one or more.

EXTENSION

Look carefully at the endings of the words in the box.
They all have an **l** sound.
Sort them into eight sets with three words in each set.
The first one is done to help you.

candle fossil hostile casual gravel cattle total nostril kestrel tonsil agile cradle battle factual postal novel cockerel rattle travel needle mental actual fertile scoundrel

1 fossil   nostril   tonsil

trans
tele
bi

Years ago, **tele**grams were **trans**ported by people on **bi**cycles.

FOCUS

KEY WORDS

- bicycle
- biplane
- biceps
- bisect
- bifocals

- telephone
- television
- telescope
- telephoto
- telepathy

- transmit
- transport
- transplant
- transparent

A Look at these picture clues. Match a key word to each.

1 _____

2 _____

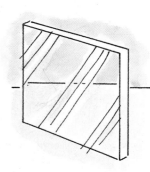

3 _____

4 _____

5 _____

6 _____

B Write three sentences. Each sentence must use one of the key words beginning with **bi**, **tele** or **trans** that you did not use in A.

A Copy the words into your book and write the definition next to the word.

1 bisect   2 bilingual   3 bifocal
4 telegraph   5 telepathy   6 television
7 transatlantic   8 translate   9 transparent

Use a dictionary for help.

B From the information in A, write what you think each of these prefixes means.

1 bi   2 tele   3 trans

XTENSION

Remember, prefixes extend or change the meanings of root words, and are important in the English language.
Remembering the main prefixes can help to improve your spelling.

A Here is a table of some frequently used prefixes with their meanings. Some prefixes have more than one meaning.

prefix	meaning	examples
con	together	convene
de	down	descend
inter	between	intervene
ob	open, clear	obvious
ob	against	object
pre	before	precaution
re	again, back	reappear
un	not	unimportant

Copy this table neatly into your book. Add some other examples.

B Compose a sentence with as many words as possible that have prefixes.

adding
S
or
es

puppies · dog · foxes · boys · elephants

FOCUS

KEY WORDS

dog
dogs
elephant
elephants
dish
dishes
fox
foxes
baby
babies
boy
boys
knife
knives

A Copy and finish the phrase to describe each of these pictures.
The first one is done to help you.

dog   **elephant**   **baby**

1 a pack of *dogs*   2 a herd of ___   3 twin ___

dish   **knife**   **boy**

4 a stack of ___   5 three sharp ___   6 a gang of ___

B Write a word that rhymes with each of these words, and has the same
spelling pattern.

1 boys   2 dishes   3 rays   4 knives   5 guppies

24

Remember, when we speak or write about **only one** thing it is **singular**.
When we talk about **two or more** things they are **plural**.
We usually add **s** or **es**.

singular	plural
elephant + s	= elephant**s**
dish + **es**	= dish**es**

Remember,
we add **es** if a word ends
with **s**, **x**, **ch** or **sh**.

A Write the plural of these words.

1 school 2 bike 3 toothbrush 4 fox 5 pass
6 splash 7 watch 8 aeroplane 9 crash 10 mouse

Remember, to make a noun plural that ends with a **y**, change
the **y** to **i** before adding **es**.

singular	plural
story	stor**ies**

But if the letter before the **y** is a vowel letter (**a e i o u**), simply add **s**.

| toy | toy**s** |
| trolley | trolley**s** |

B Copy this table. Make the plurals of these nouns.

singular	monkey	cry	nappy	turkey	hobby	baby	chimney	jockey
plural								

Remember, we often add **s** or **es** to make a verb singular, but the same
spelling rules apply.

they run   he run**s**   they hurry   she hurr**ies**

Remember,
most **verbs** are
action words.

Make these verbs singular. Use each one in a sentence.
The first one is done to help you.

1 **terrify** terrifies The loud noise terrifies the kitten.

2 hurry   3 jump   4 bury   5 defy
6 copy   7 watch   8 wash   9 marry

25

CHECK-UP 1

A Look at these pictures and clues.
Write the words in your book.

1 a circle's outer edge

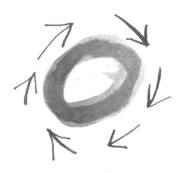

c_____

2 another name for a car

a_____

3 a breed of dog

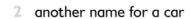

c_____

4 a small bunch of flowers

p_____

5 can last for long periods
without water

c_____

6 used to see long distances

t_____

B Write the answers to these clues in your book.

1 a synonym for frightened   s_____

2 one before second   f_____

3 what people do when they finish their working life   r_____

4 the antonym of appear   d_____

A Copy and complete these word wheels in your book.

impress

press

pressed

enjoy

joy

B Write the plural form of each of these nouns.

1 *domino* 2 *cuckoo* 3 *photo* 4 *piano*

C Write a definition for each of these words.

1 discard 2 disappear 3 dislocate 4 disclose

D The answers to these clues end with the letter pattern **el**.

1 a male chicken
2 a bird of prey that can hover
3 a sharp tool used by carpenters
4 a synonym for gem

EXTENSION

A Make new words by adding a different suffix to each of these words.

1 *smart* 2 *scare* 3 *art* 4 *care*

B Write a definition for each of these words.

1 acquire 2 circumvent 3 expire 4 autobiography

C Write the plurals of these words.

1 *baby* 2 *day* 3 *posy* 4 *berry* 5 *puppy*

D Write two words that begin with each of these prefixes.

1 *con* (meaning *together*) 2 *inter* (meaning *between*)
3 *pre* (meaning *before*) 4 *re* (meaning *again*)

OW
endings

sparrow

hollow

burrow

shadow

FOCUS

KEY WORDS

arrow
narrow
sparrow
yellow
elbow
pillow
window
follow
hollow
borrow
sorrow
burrow
shadow
shallow

A Copy these groups of words.
Underline the word in each group with the different letter pattern.

1 pillow   willow   shadow   billow
2 narrow   follow   sparrow   arrow
3 elbow   shallow   swallow   allow

B What am I?
Look at the picture clues and complete the sentences.
Then find the key word that matches the clue. The first one is done to help you.

1 Rest your on me. *pillow*

2 I am a small brown .

3 I'm home to a family of  .

4 When the shines I never leave your side.

5 Mix me with and I turn green.

EXTRA

growl	known	prowl	show

growth scowl clown slow blown
brown throw crown shown down
frown thrown

Sort the words in the box into sound pattern families, like this:

words with <u>ow</u> sounding like c<u>ow</u>	words with <u>ow</u> sounding like wind<u>ow</u>
clown	slow

Write a sentence using one word from each family.

EXTENSION

Remember, a syllable is a part of a word that can be sounded by itself. Each syllable has its own vowel sound. For example:

pillow **pil/low** two syllables
arrow **ar/row** also two syllables.

grow follow following rainbow
window swallow tomorrow barrow
own mower borrowing hollow

Does each of your **syllables** have a **vowel sound**?

Sort the words in the box into lists of one-syllable, two-syllable and three-syllable words, like this:

one syllable	two syllables	three syllables
grow	follow = fol/low	following = fol/low/ing

et

endings

Put your money in the bucket
For a packet full of tickets
For a ride in the rocket.
Guaranteed fun!

FOCUS

KEY WORDS

jacket
packet
racket

ticket
wicket
cricket
thicket

locket
pocket
rocket
socket

bucket

A Each of these key word has had its vowel letters (**a e i o u**) taken out. Write the words in your book.

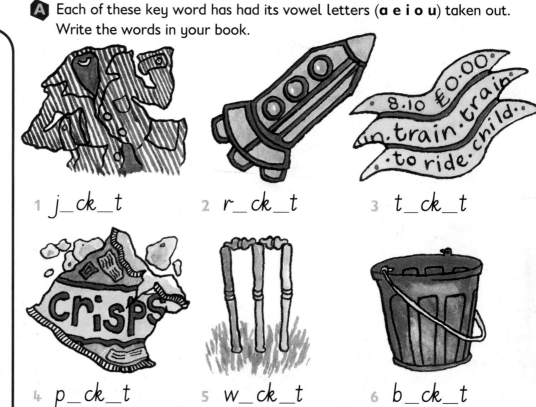

1 j_ck_t

2 r_ck_t

3 t_ck_t

4 p_ck_t

5 w_ck_t

6 b_ck_t

B What am I?

1 I'm used in tennis and rhyme with **packet**.
2 I allow you to travel and rhyme with **thicket**.
3 I launch satellites and rhyme with **socket**.
4 I'm a game and rhyme with **wicket**.
5 I carry your money and rhyme with **locket**.

EXTRA

A Look carefully at these words.
Copy them into your book, and underline the one that has a different letter pattern.

1 magnet cabinet tablet bonnet

2 wicket helmet cricket bucket packet

3 upset droplet triplet pellet bullet

4 socket locket ticket gadget racket

EXTENSION

Remember, a **syllable** is a part of a word that can be said by itself.
Each syllable has its own vowel sound.

let   **let**   one syllable
blanket   **blan/ket**   two syllables

Copy these words. Put a line between the syllables.

1 gadget   2 met   3 velvet   4 regret

5 regrettable   6 filleted   7 upsetting   8 bullet

9 puppet   10 trumpeting   11 pocket

ull
ul

A **bull** on a farm
Can do no harm.
A **bull** in a china shop–
Be care**ful**!

 **F** OCUS

KEY WORDS

bull
full
pull
dull
gull
bully
fully
gully
helpfully
painful
usefully
beautifully

A Match a key word to each picture clue.

1 _____

2 _____

3 _____

4 _____

B Neatly copy into your book five words that have the **fully** pattern. The key words will help you.

C Write a sentence using one of your **fully** words.

EXTRA

The suffix **ful** may be added to the end of some words to make an adjective, like this:

    help   help**ful**   use   use**ful**

Notice that it only has one **l.**

Remember, an **adjective** is a **describing word**.

Add a **ful** suffix to make these words into adjectives.

  1 shame 2 deceit   3 spite 4 pain 5 hope

  6 wonder 7 thought 8 care 9 sorrow

EXTENSION

If you are adding the suffix **ful** to a word ending in **y**, remember to change **y** to **i** first, like this:

    plenty   plent**iful**

A Add a **ful** suffix to make these words into adjectives.

  1 beauty   2 duty 3 fancy 4 mercy

B Use a word with the **ful** suffix to fill the gaps when you write these sentences.
The word in bold is a clue.

  1 **beauty** It was a _____ park.

  2 **shame** Everyone said it was _____ when it was dug up for a new road.

  3 **dread** They made a _____ mess and noise.

  4 **hope** We are _____ that the traffic won't cause too many accidents .

soft

C

I think mice
Are rather nice...
No one seems to like them much.
But I think mice
Are nice.

Rose Fyleman

 OCUS

KEY WORDS

city
circus
centre
cereal
certain
cycle

ace
face
race

recent
concert
December

except
excellent

A Read the poem.
Nice and **mice** have a **c** that sounds like **s**. We say it is 'soft'.
Find eleven **soft c** words hidden in the puzzle box.
Six start with a **soft c** and five have a **soft c** somewhere else.

c	d	l	e	g	z	x	c
e	f	a	c	y	c	l	e
r	a	c	e	c	f	y	r
e	c	e	n	t	r	e	t
a	e	c	i	t	y	b	a
l	e	x	c	e	p	t	i
c	e	m	e	n	t	a	n

B Write in your book the key words that have both a **soft c** and a **hard c**.

| office | dice | rice | police |
| price | mice | twice | notice |

Match an **ice** word from the box with each clue.
The first one is done to help you.

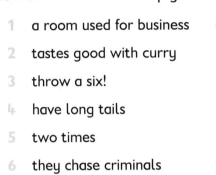

1   a room used for business   *office*

2   tastes good with curry

3   throw a six!

4   have long tails

5   two times

6   they chase criminals

7   gives information

8   can be cheap, can be expensive

EXTENSION

ace is another common **soft c** letter pattern.

A Make a list of words with **ace** in them, using the word fan.

pl
tr
p
p   pal
r
l
f
sp
firepl

+ ace

Don't forget, if more
than one word has the
same first letter, look at
the next letters.

B Put the words you have made in alphabetical order.

35

homophones

Ratty and Mole **rowed** down the river in the **tale** *The Wind in the Willows* by Kenneth Grahame.

KEY WORDS

rain
rein
reign
dear
deer
knight
night
not
knot
flour
flower
sun
son

Look at these picture clues.
Write the correct key word in your book.

1 _____

2 _____

3 _____

4 _____

5 _____

6 _____

> Remember, **homophones** are words that sound the same, but which are spelt differently.
> We passed **two beech** trees as we walked **to** the **beach** to **see** the **sea**.

A Write a homophone for each of these words.

1	ewe	2	maid	3	blew	4	here
5	our	6	vain	7	board	8	cereal
9	quay	10	weak	11	to	12	leek

B Write sentences about a trip to the beach using four of the pairs of homophones in A.

XTENSION

> **Mnemonics** (pronounced *nemonics*) are short phrases or rhymes that help us remember things. We can use mnemonics to help us to remember which homophone to use.
>
> **hear** or **here**   We <u>hear</u> with our <u>ear</u>.   It's <u>here</u> not t<u>here</u>.

A Copy these words and phrases. Underline the letters in each that the mnemonic helps us to remember.

1 beach or beech The beach is by the sea.

2 heard or herd I heard with my ear.

3 steel or steal Dad tried to steal Mum's cup of tea.

4 meet or meat We can eat meat.

B Make up your own mnemonics to help you remember which of these homophones to use.

1 serial or cereal   2 stair or stare

3 hair or hare   4 board or bored

unstressed vowels

FOCUS

KEY WORDS

family
different
generally
marvellous
generous
interesting
miserable
boundary
factory
separate
listener
easily
lottery

A How many words can you find hidden in the puzzle box?
Copy them into your book.

x	m	a	r	v	e	l	l	o	u	s	n
d	i	c	t	i	o	n	a	r	y	t	b
i	s	e	p	a	r	a	t	e	f	a	b
f	e	a	s	i	l	y	u	y	f	t	f
f	r	g	e	n	e	r	a	l	a	i	a
e	a	n	i	m	a	l	f	d	c	o	m
r	b	o	u	n	d	a	r	y	t	n	i
e	l	i	s	t	e	n	e	r	o	a	l
n	e	l	o	t	t	e	r	y	r	r	y
t	x	e	f	n	e	p	d	j	y	y	s

B Put a tick next to each of the key words in your list.

38

Unstressed vowels are vowel letters which we either do not sound, or do not sound very distinctly, as we speak. Unstressed vowels can cause spelling problems because it is easy to forget them and miss them out.

int<u>e</u>resting

interesting sounds like *intresting*, because the **e** is an unstressed vowel.

A Copy these words. Circle the unstressed vowels.

1 conference   2 library   3 offering

4 explanatory   5 temperature   6 dictionary

7 vegetables   8 literacy   9 voluntary

B Use a dictionary to help you spot the unstressed vowels that have been left out of these words. Write the words correctly.

1 litrature   2 secretry   3 defnitely
4 necessry   5 compny   6 frightning
7 nursry   8 prisner   9 poisnous

EXTENSION

It can sometimes help to spell words correctly that have unstressed vowels, if we think of the syllables.

Remember, every syllable needs a vowel sound.
desperate   **des / per / ate**
This reminds us not to spell the word *desprate*.

Remember,
the letter **y** can make a
vowel sound.

Copy each of these words into your book, saying them quietly to yourself as you do. Next to each word write its syllables. The first one is done to help you.

1 jewellery   jew/el/lery

2 freedom   3 deafening   4 catholic

5 widening   6 flattery   7 abandoned

8 abominable   9 originally   10 occasionally

ost
oll

You alm**ost** missed the **post** by str**oll**ing down the road.

FOCUS

KEY WORDS

post
host
ghost
most
almost
roll
toll
troll
stroll
scroll
swollen

A Look at these picture clues.
Write the **ost** or **oll** words in your book.

1 p_____

2 h_____

3 t_____

4 s_____

B 1 Write two words that rhyme with **cost**. The first letters will give you a clue.

l _____   fr _____

2 Write three words that rhyme with **most**.

3 Write four words that rhyme with **toll**.

EXTRA

The letter patterns **oll**, **oal** and **ole** usually make the same sound.
Look at the clues and the first letters of these words. Each word needs one of the letter patterns. Write the answers in your book.

Use a dictionary to check your answers.

1 f_____   a young horse

2 r_____   small type of bread

3 h_____   space left after something is taken out

4 c_____   black lumps that burn

5 st_____   a gentle walk

6 st_____   what the thief did

7 p_____   often has a flag at the top

8 sh_____   large group of fish

EXTENSION

Say these words quietly to yourself:

  also almost   ball tall

Notice that when the **al** pattern comes at the beginning of a word it is usually spelt with one **l**, but when it comes at the end of a word it is often spelt with two.

All right
is always **two** words!

A Add **all** or **al** to make these words. If you are unsure of any, check them in a dictionary.

1 ____ so   2 ____ ready   3 sm____

4 f____   5 ____ together   6 ____ ways

7 st____   8 ____ mighty   9 ____ though

B Put the words you have made in alphabetical order. Remember to look at the third, or even fourth, letter.

UNIT 18

same letters different sound

> What on **ear**th shall we w**ear**?
> I f**ear** we will be late!

FOCUS

KEY WORDS

bear
fear
earth
light
eight
weight
bought
bough
shield
lie
pie
your
our
flour

A Write the rhyming words.
The picture clue will help you.

pear	**rear**	**freight**

1 _____ 2 _____ 3 _____

night	**tie**	**hour**

4 _____ 5 _____ 6 _____

B Add another word yourself that rhymes with and has the same spelling pattern as each of the words you have written.

EXTRA

Some letter patterns have more than one sound. For example:
the gr**ea**t b**ea**st's h**ea**d

A 1 Draw a table and sort the words in the box into lists according to the sound the **ea** pattern makes. Some words go in more than one list.

weather jealously read heater break treasure measuring streak meat
seating reader bread steak greater lead beating greatly heavenly

ea sounds like e in hen	ea sounds like ai in pain	ea sounds like ee in feet
weather	break	streak

2 Which of the words in the box went into more than one list?

B 1 From your reading book, find and copy six words that have an **ea** pattern. Next to each word you have copied, write two others that have an **ea** pattern that makes the same sound.

2 In **lie** and **field**, **ie** has a different sound. Write four words with an **ie** pattern and sound similar to **lie**, and four words with an **ie** pattern that makes a sound similar to **field**.

EXTENSION

A Sort the words in Box A into lists according to the sound the **ear** makes.

Box A

earn year dear learn yearn beard
search near heard gear earth rear

Beware!
In Box B two of the words are in lists by themselves.

B Sort the words in Box B into lists according to the sound the **ough** makes.

Box B

bough thought plough wrought bought
enough though brought drought sought

Using a dictionary

motto *n.* an inspiring saying or slogan, such as 'never yield' (*pl.* **mottoes**).

mould (1) *n.* mildew, a fungus growing in damp places. *adj.* **mouldy**.

mould (2) *n.* 1. a hollow shape into which molten metal is poured to cast it into a shape. 2. a similar mould for jellies.

moulding *n.* 1. something moulded. 2. an ornament on a building.

moult *v.* for animals or birds to cast off fur or feathers at certain seasons. *n.* **moult** the seasonal shedding of fur or feathers by certain animals or birds.

mound *n.* a heap of earth or stones, a small hill.

mount *v.* 1. to climb, as *to mount stairs*. 2. to get on to, as *to mount a horse*. 3. to fix, as *to mount a picture on cardboard*. *n.* **mount** 1. a high hill. 2. a cardboard backing for a picture. 3. a horse for riding.

mountain *n.* a very high hill *adj.* **mountainous** having many mountains. *n.* **mountaineer** a person who climbs mountains.

mourn *v.* to feel deep sorrow. *adj.* **mournful** sorrowful. *n.* **mourner** someone at a funeral.

in mourning dressed in funeral clothes.

mouse *n.* a small, long-tailed gnawing animal (*pl.* **mice**). *adj.* **mousy** like a mouse.

moustache *n.* hair on a man's top lip.

mouth *n.* 1. the opening in the head for speaking and eating. 2. any opening, as *the mouth of a river or cave* (*pl.* **mouths** *pron.* mowTHz). *n.* **mouthful** (*pl.* **mouthfuls**).

down in the mouth down-hearted.

living from hand to mouth living from day to day not saving anything.

F **OCUS**

KEY WORDS

letters
words
vowel
consonant
order
alphabet
dictionary
definition
origin
meaning
guide
abbreviation

a b c d e f g h i j k l m n o p q r s t u v w x y z

The words in a dictionary are arranged in alphabetical order. Write each of these lists of words in alphabetical order.

1 animal house mother bicycle river

2 bingo below battery blend bulrushes

3 department favourite distance flavour dutiful

4 package paper palm padlock panel

5 strike struggle stroke stream stranger

6 transparent transport transmitter translation transfusion

EXTRA

Dictionaries enable us to check the spelling of a word.

Dictionaries contain lots of information about each word:
- its definition
- what word class (part of speech) it is
  (n = noun; v = verb; adj = adjective)
- its origin, in some cases
- related words or sayings, if it has any.

Use the pages from the dictionary on the facing page to help you answer the following questions.

A Write these words, spelling them correctly.

mold   mountin   mountainus   mustarsh

B 1 Which word comes between **mount** and **mourn**?
  2 Which word follows **mound**?
  3 What class of word is **mountainous**?
  4 What is a **motto**?
  5 What does **down in the mouth** mean?
  6 What are the two quite different meanings of **mould**?
  7 What is the plural of **mouse**?
  8 What is the plural of **motto**?

EXTENSION

At the top of each page are **guide words**, which are the first and last words on that page. The guide words on the page opposite are MOTTO and MOUTH.

Here are the guide words from three different pages in the dictionary.

COOL – CORRESPOND p42
CORRESPONDENT – COUNTRY p43
IMPULSE – INDEPENDENT p109

A Write the number of the page on which the following words would appear.

1 coroner   2 count   3 increase   4 inadequate   5 copper
6 correspond   7 incident   8 indeed   9 core   10 cosmonaut
11 corrupt   12 income   13 coppice   14 inadvertent   15 council

B What are the guide words on the page in your own dictionary on which these words appear?

1 slick   2 possum   3 microscope   4 immune   5 constituency
6 emu   7 detect   8 incredible   9 natural   10 valiant
11 frantic   12 thistle   13 diamond   14 bottle   15 feeble

OCUS

A What are these? One letter is given to help you.
Write the words in your book.

1 p_____

2 _n_____

3 _r_____

4 r_____

5 c_____

6 _____l

7 r_____

8 _a_____

9 p_____

10 ___g_____

11 s_____

12 _i_____

B Write a word that rhymes with each of these words, and has the same
spelling pattern.

1 toys   2 dishes   3 guppies   4 wives

A Copy these words into your book, and underline the odd-one-out in each set that has a different letter pattern.

1 cabinet wicket bonnet magnet
2 inset droplet hamlet pellet wallet
3 ticket locket gadget racket socket

B Write an **ice** or **ace** word for each clue.
1 a royal residence
2 tastes good with curry
3 furry little creatures which have long tails
4 front of the head
5 two times

C Write a homophone for each of these words.
1 you   2 blue   3 there   4 cereal
5 key   6 week   7 threw   8 mite

D Copy these words. Circle the unstressed vowels.

1 different   2 dictionary   3 temperature
4 vegetables   5 lottery   6 Wednesday

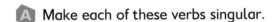

XTENSION

A Make each of these verbs singular.

1 wash   2 terrify   3 jump
4 copy   5 defy   6 hurry

B Copy these words. Then next to each write the syllables.

1 window   2 borrow   3 swallowing
4 rainbow   5 throw   6 growing

C Add a **ful** suffix to make these words into adjectives.

1 shame   2 deceit   3 duty
4 beauty   5 mercy   6 help

D Add **all** or **al** to complete these words.

1 ____ways   2 st____   3 ____together
4 h____   5 ____most   6 ____mighty

un
en
in
im

KEY WORDS

undone
unhappy
unkind
untidy

enable
enclose
enlarge

inaccurate
incomplete
incorrect
invisible

imperfect
impossible
impure

A Match a key word to each of these pictures.
Write the answers in your book.

1 un_____ 2 un_____ 3 en _____

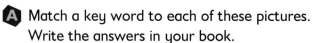

4 in_____ 5 in_____ 6 im_____

B Write sentences using two of these words.

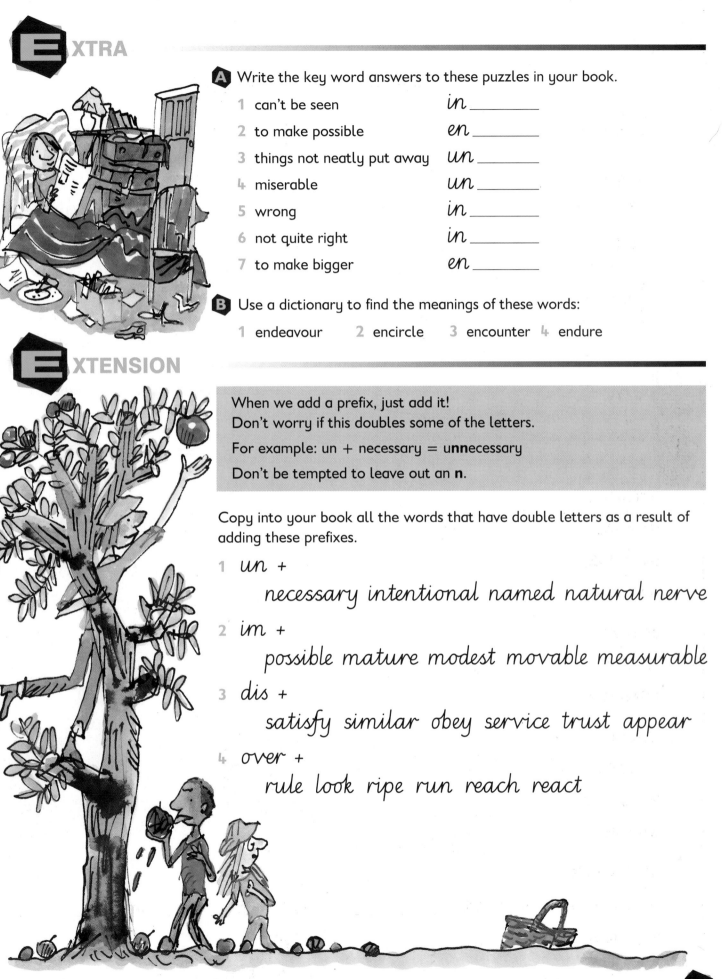

EXTRA

A Write the key word answers to these puzzles in your book.

1 can't be seen   *in* _____

2 to make possible   *en* _____

3 things not neatly put away   *un* _____

4 miserable   *un* _____

5 wrong   *in* _____

6 not quite right   *in* _____

7 to make bigger   *en* _____

B Use a dictionary to find the meanings of these words:

1 endeavour   2 encircle   3 encounter   4 endure

EXTENSION

When we add a prefix, just add it!
Don't worry if this doubles some of the letters.

For example: un + necessary = u**nn**ecessary

Don't be tempted to leave out an **n**.

Copy into your book all the words that have double letters as a result of adding these prefixes.

1 *un +*
     necessary intentional named natural nerve

2 *im +*
     possible mature modest movable measurable

3 *dis +*
     satisfy similar obey service trust appear

4 *over +*
     rule look ripe run reach react

soft
g

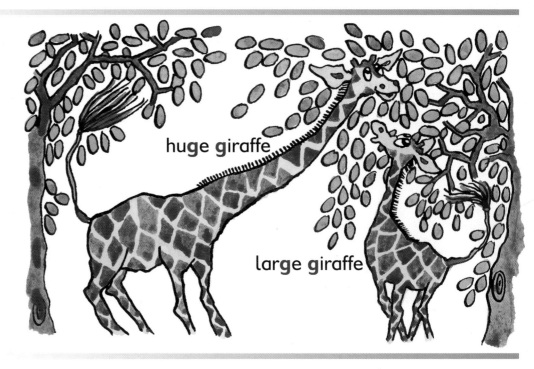

huge giraffe

large giraffe

 FOCUS

KEY WORDS

gem
gentle
general
giraffe

age
angel
urgent
danger
larger
tragic
huge

A Write a key word to go with each picture.

1 _____   2 _____   3 _____

4 _____   5 _____   6 _____

B Write key words that have similar meanings to these.

1 needed in a hurry   2 bigger
3 very big   4 valuable stone

EXTRA

Hidden in the puzzle are ten words which have the **age** letter pattern.

b	d	x	o	p	c						
p	a	g	e	v	a	m	p	a	c	k	a	g	e
v	m	o	l	i	b	c	o	t	t	a	g	e	t
o	a	t	y	l	b	r	w	a	g	e	s	l	o
y	g	n	c	l	a	d	v	a	n	t	a	g	e
a	e	p	z	a	g						
g	a	r	a	g	e						
e	x	j	y	e	f						

A Write the ten words in your book.
Try to add more **age** words to your list.

B Write a sentence that uses your shortest **age** word, and a sentence using your longest.

EXTENSION

A **definition** is
a meaning of a word.

> range hinge fringe sponge plunge strange orange

All the words in the box have the **nge** letter pattern.
In this table, some of the words are missing and some of the definitions are missing. Copy and complete the table in your book. Use a dictionary to help you.

fringe	hair cut low across the forehead
range	
	metal joint on which a door swings
sponge	
	a dive
strange	
	a citrus fruit

ie

Good grief!
Would you bel**ie**ve it?

FOCUS

KEY WORDS

brief
grief
chief
thief
frieze
priest
field
shield
belief
believe
relief
relieve

A Find ten **ie** key words hidden in the box.

b	i	k	j	g	e	f	s
h	f	b	p	r	d	r	h
g	r	e	r	i	c	i	i
b	e	l	i	e	v	e	e
r	l	i	e	f	l	z	l
i	i	e	s	a	m	e	d
e	e	f	t	h	i	e	f
f	f	i	e	l	d	n	o

B Write the answers to this quiz in your book.
All the answers are **ie** words.

1 What is another name for a robber?

2 What is the leader of a group of people called?

3 What is great sadness?

4 What does a warrior carry for protection?

 **XTRA**

To make plurals from nouns that end in **f** or **fe**, we usually change the **f** to **v** and add **es**, like this:

one thief, two thie**ves**   one life, two li**ves**.

Sometimes, but not often, we simply add **s**, like this:

one chief, two chie**fs**.

Copy these words. Next to each one, write its plural and a sentence with the word in it. The first one is done to help you. They all, except one, need the **f** to be changed.

1 *thief thieves   The thieves stole my bike.*
2 *loaf*   3 *wolf*   4 *shelf*   5 *leaf*
6 *chief*   7 *life*   8 *knife*   9 *wife*

E **XTENSION**

A **view** is a root word for many other words.
Draw a word wheel and add as many words containing **view** as you can. Here are some to get you started.

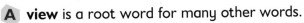

view   *viewing*

interview

Don't forget you can add prefixes (like **inter** and **re**) or suffixes (like **er**, **ed** and **ing**) or both to build the words.

B Can you think of another word to use at the centre of a word wheel? Make a wheel of your own.

ei

All the **eights**
eighty-eight!

FOCUS

KEY WORDS

eight
eighteen
eighty
eightieth
reins
vein
reign
sleigh
weigh
weight
freight
neighbour
height
either

A Which key word do you think of when you look at these pictures?

1 _____   2 _____   3 _____

B Write down the twelve key words you can find hidden in this letter jumble. Some letters are used more than once, and some words can be found more than once.

v	t	r	s	i	e	r	e	y
f	g	f	l	e	i	s	i	v
i	s	h	e	i	g	h	t	e
e	r	e	i	t	h	r	w	i
w	e	i	g	h	t	e	e	n
e	i	g	h	e	y	i	i	y
g	g	h	a	r	x	n	g	o
h	n	t	s	l	a	s	h	n
f	f	r	e	i	g	h	t	l

This rule will help you to remember whether the **i** comes before or after the **e**.

i comes before **e**	– p**ie**ce, rel**ie**f
except after **c**	– rec**ei**ve, c**ei**ling
or when the sound is not **ee**	– forf**ei**t, r**ei**gn

1 Copy these words into your book.

> *receive their sleight field deceit*
> *leisure believe rein achieve wield chief*
> *shield vein eight receipt*

2 Tick the words in which the **ie** or the **ei** sounds **ee**.
3 Underline those you have ticked that have an **ei**.
4 What do you notice about the words you have underlined?
5 What do you notice about the words you have not underlined or ticked?

Look at the sets of homophones in the box.
Choose three sets and use your dictionary to find out what each word means.
Write the definitions in your book. The first one is done to help you.

Homophones
sound the same but have different spellings and meanings.

> *reign weigh eight weight sleigh vein ate*
> *rein way wait slay vane rain vain*

rein　　　　　*reign*　　　　　*rain*

ey
endings

I met a mon**key**.
We had tea.
Toast and hon**ey**
All over me!

FOCUS

KEY WORDS

abbey
alley
valley
donkey
monkey
honey
money
jockey
trolley
chimney
chutney
turkey
journey

A Copy these groups of words.
Underline the one with the different letter pattern.

1 monkey chutney donkey turkey
2 jockey money chimney honey
3 alley abbey valley trolley

B What am I?
Look at the picture clues and complete the sentences.
Then find the key word that matches the clue.

1 I race  . *jockey*

2 I'm very good at climbing .

3 I sit on top of a  .

4 I'm made by  .

5 You need me to buy  .

EXTRA

Remember,
a **noun**
is a **naming word**.

Remember, when we add **s** to most words that end with **y**, we change the **y** to **i** and add **es**, like this:

one lolly   three loll**ies**

But if the word ends in a **vowel** (**a e i o u**) + **y**, we simply add **s**, like this:

one monk**ey**   three monk**eys**

Make these nouns plural.

1 toy	2 trolley	3 lady	4 fly
5 chimney	6 jockey	7 runaway	8 guy
9 difficulty	10 valley	11 activity	12 injury
13 boy	14 donkey	15 battery	16 monkey

EXTENSION

Look again at the rules in Extra. If we need to add **s** to a verb, the same spelling rules apply.

Copy these sentences and write a verb ending in **s** to fill each gap. The word in brackets will help you.

"That new puppy always (defy) me!" shouted Dad. "I think he (try) to make me mad! Who (pay) for all the new plants – him or me?"

"Dad always (fly) into a rage when Spot (bury) his bone in the vegetable patch."

ild
ind

In the labyrinth,
Paths twist and w**ind**.
Answer the riddles.
What will you **find**?

FOCUS

KEY WORDS

mild
wild
child
bind
find
kind
mind
wind
blind
grind

A Look at the picture.
Copy these sentences, filling in the gaps with key words.

"I can't f____ my way," said the woman.

"Would you m ____ helping me?" she asked.

"No, I don't m____," said the c____.

"You are very k ____," said the woman with a smile.

B Copy these groups of words. Underline the word in each group with the different letter pattern.

1 mild   wild   find   child   children

2 kind   grind   pint   find   wind

3 grind   ground   mind   bind   minder

Words that are spelt the same and sound the same but have different meanings are called **homonyms**.

Look at the two pictures below.

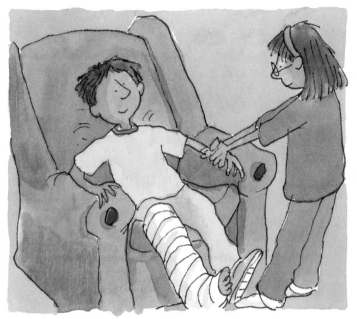

She was very **kind** to her brother.

What **kind** of dog do you like best?

Write two sentences for each of these words to show they can have two different meanings.

1 bank   2 bow   3 bark   4 bat   5 watch

XTENSION

> We sometimes add prefixes to the beginning and suffixes to the end of words, like this:
>
> **unkindness**
>
> prefix   root word   suffix

Copy these words into your book. Underline the root word of each.

1 remind   2 unwinding   3 rewinding   4 unkindly

5 children   6 minder   7 grinding   8 wilderness

9 blindingly   10 reminds   11 childish   12 kindness

-e or -e̶?

shake   shaking   smile   smiling

OCUS

KEY WORDS

shake
shaking
shaker

cure
curing
curable

close
closing
closed

ride
riding

smile
smiling

A Match a key word ending in **ing** to each of these actions.
The first one is done to help you.

1 c_____   2 r_____

3 s_____   4 s_____

B Copy these verbs. Next to each write the family word you used in section A.

1 close   2 ride   3 smile   4 shake

C Write a sentence explaining what happens to words ending in **e** when **ing** is added.

EXTRA

Words ending in **magic e** drop the **e** when **ing** is added.

blaze blaz**ing**　　hide hid**ing**

A Copy and complete each of these word sums.

1 live + ing =　　2 save + ing =　　3 care + ing =

4 tame + ing =　　5 shame + ing =　　6 shine + ing =

7 strive + ing =　　8 slope + ing =　　9 smile + ing =

B Make up six more similar word sums yourself.

EXTENSION

Remember,
the vowel letters are
a, e, i, o and **u;**
the rest are consonants.

Words ending in **magic e** keep the **e** when a suffix that begins with a consonant is added.

hop**e** + **f**ul = hopeful　　tun**e** + **l**ess = tuneless

Words ending in **magic e** drop the **e** when a suffix that begins with a vowel is added.

cur**e** + **a**ble = curable　　jok**e** + **e**r = joker

A Write in your book as many words as you can combining the root words with the suffixes from the vowel suffix box and the consonant suffix box.

Root words
use recognise combine rehearse scribble response believe improve excite like hope sense age large

Vowel suffixes
able ing ed er est ible al ism

Consonant suffixes
ly ful ment less

B Skim through some books and list other root words ending in **e** that use each of the suffixes in the two suffix boxes.

CHECK-UP 3

OCUS

A Look at these clues.
Write the words in your book.

1 a bright flame lit by ships in distress   f _____
2 needing a drink   th _____
3 entertainment under the Big Top   c _____
4 smoke and flames   f _____
5 machine that works by itself   a _____
6 the antonym of trust   d _____
7 Australian animal with a long hop   k _____
8 used for drying oneself   t _____
9 used for speaking over long distances   t _____
10 someone who steals   th _____

B What are these? One letter is given to help you.
Write the words in your book.

1 j _____
2 __i_____
3 __h_____
4 __g_____

5 c _____
6 f _____
7 __i_____
8 f _____

C Write a word that rhymes with each of these words, and has the same spelling pattern.

1 bays   2 crosses   3 cherries   4 leaves

D Write each of these lists of words in alphabetical order.

1 confirm conduct concert consider
2 habit harvest hound handle hawk hedge

EXTRA

A List four words based on these root words.

1 wonder   2 hope   3 care

B Write the plural form of each of these words.

1 cello   2 kangaroo   3 hippo

4 potato   5 wife   6 difficulty

7 trolley   8 activity   9 thief

C Copy these words into your book, and underline the word in each set that has a different letter pattern.

1 packet rocket gadget racket socket

2 money jockey chimney honey

3 alley abbey valley trolley

4 bind mild child wild

D Write two sentences for each of these homonyms to show that they can have more than one meaning.

1 clip   2 catch   3 bank

E Write an **ice** or **ace** word for each clue.

1 for fastening a shoe
2 a room for business
3 officers in uniform who keep the peace
4 cubes with numbers for playing board games
5 a running competition

F Write a homophone for each of these words.

1 air   2 right   3 here   4 rows

5 bow   6 course   7 flower   8 plain

G Copy these words. Circle the unstressed vowels.

1 desperate   2 jewellery   3 Wednesday

4 explanatory   5 lottery   6 similar

A Write a definition for each of these words.

1 incapable   2 circulate   3 bisect   4 telepathy

B Write two words that begin with each of these prefixes.

1 *auto* (meaning *self*)   2 *circum* (meaning *round*)

3 *bi* (meaning *two*)   4 *tele* (meaning *across*)

C Make each of these verbs singular.

1 *push*   2 *horrify*   3 *skip*   4 *marry*   5 *imply*

D Copy these words. Then next to each write the syllables.

1 *grateful*   2 *gratitude*   3 *unnecessarily*

4 *inconsiderately*   5 *thoughtfully*

E Add a **ful** suffix to make these words into adjectives.

1 *thank*   2 *mercy*   3 *doubt*   4 *pity*

F Add **all** or **al** to complete these words.

1 ___*though*   2 *t*_____   3 ___*ways*   4 *sh*_____

G What are the guide words on the page in your own dictionary on which these words appear?

1 hostel   2 estuary   3 sleigh   4 possible   5 spy

H What is the mistake being made by the person writing these words?

unecessary unatural disimilar imature overule

I Write in your book as many words as you can combining the root words with the suffixes from the vowel suffix box and the consonant suffix box.

Root words
suit rely happy cheer argue post scribble
response sense large critic

Vowel suffixes
able ing ed er est
ible al ism ably

Consonant suffixes
ly ful ment less ness